CIVIL WAR CHRONICLES

GETTYSBURG

By Ruth Ashby

For Ernie —R.A.

Published by iBooks
an imprint of J. Boylston & Company, Publishers

Published by iBooks an imprint of
J. Boylston & Company, Publishers
Produced by Byron Preiss Visual Publications, Inc.
Manhanset House
POB 342
Dering Harbor NY 11965
bricktower@aol.com • www.ibooksinc.com

Produced by Byron Preiss Visual Publications, Inc.

Library of Congress Cataloging-in-Publication Data
Ashby, Ruth.
Gettysburg / by Ruth Ashby
v. cm. — (Civil War Chronicles)

ISBN 978-1-59687-724-5
1. Gettysburg (pa.) Battle of, 1863—Juvenile literature. 2. United States—History—Civil War, 1861-1865—Campaigns.] I. Title.

E450 .A84 2002
973.7'115—dc21 2002017638

December 2025

Contents

Introduction

The Civil War was the great American tragedy. From 1861 to 1865, it divided states, broke up families, took the lives of more than half a million people, and left much of the country in ruins. But it also abolished the great national shame of slavery and cleared the way for the astounding expansion of American industry and culture in the second half of the 19th century. Without the war, the United States would not have been so progressive or so united—and millions of its people would still have been in chains. In the end it was, perhaps, a necessary tragedy.

Abraham Lincoln

The conflict had loomed for decades. From the Constitutional Convention in 1787 on, the North and South had disagreed about whether slavery should exist in the United States. In the North, slavery was gradually abolished between 1780 and 1827. But the South became ever more yoked to slavery as its economy became more dependent on the production of cotton. In the meantime, the United States was expanding westward. Every time a territory became a new state, the government had to decide whether it would be slave or free. For 40 years, Congress reached compromise after compromise.

Jefferson Davis

Finally, differences could no longer be bandaged over. With the election of Republican Abraham Lincoln to the presidency in 1860, a crisis was reached. Southern states were afraid that Lincoln, who opposed slavery in the territories, would try to abolish it in the South as well—and that their economy and way of life would be destroyed. On December 20, 1860, South Carolina seceded from the Union. It was

Robert E. Lee 

Ulysses S. Grant

followed by Alabama, Florida, Georgia, Louisiana, Mississippi, Texas, Virginia, North Carolina, Tennessee, and Arkansas.

The rebellious states formed a new nation, the Confederate States of America, and elected a president, Jefferson Davis. On April 12, 1861, Confederate forces fired on the Federal post of Fort Sumter in Charleston Harbor—and the Civil War began. It lasted four years and touched the lives of every man, woman, and child in the nation. There were heroes on both sides, in the army and on the home front, from Union general Ulysses S. Grant and Confederate general Robert E. Lee to black leader Harriet Tubman and poet and nurse Walt Whitman. It is estimated that at least 620,000 soldiers were killed, almost as many Americans as in all other armed conflicts combined. When Lincoln issued the Emancipation Proclamation on January 1, 1863, and freed the slaves in the rebellious states, it became not just a war for reunification but a war of liberation as well.

Gettysburg gives a blow-by-blow account of the epic struggle that marked the turning point of the war—the greatest battle ever fought on American soil.

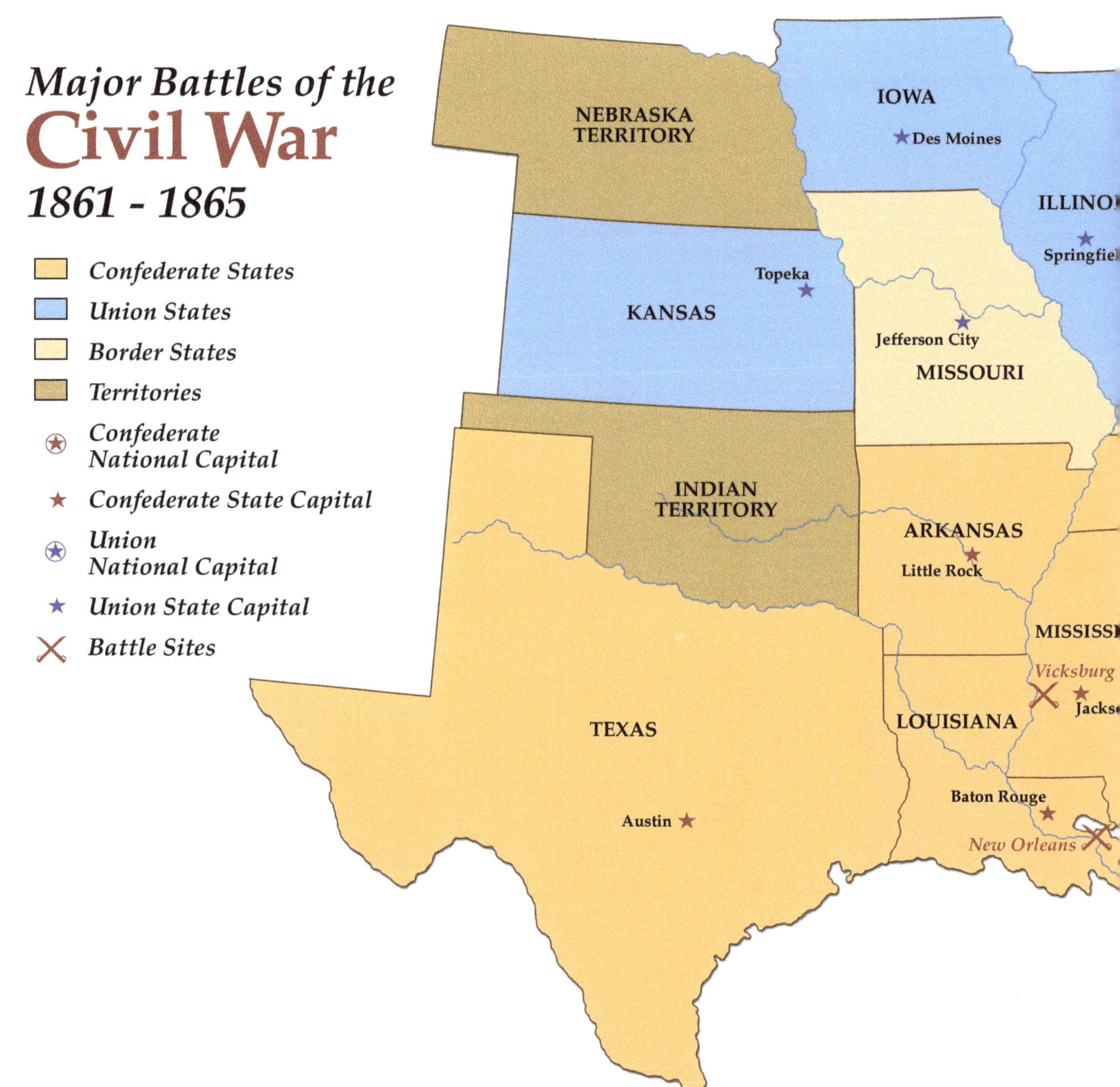

Major Battles of the
Civil War
1861 - 1865
Confederate States
Union States
Border States
Territories
Confederate National Capital
Confederate State Capital
Union National Capital
Union State Capital
Battle Sites
NEBRASKA TERRITORY
IOWA
Des Moines
KANSAS
Topeka
Jefferson City
MISSOURI
INDIAN TERRITORY
ARKANSAS
Little Rock
TEXAS
Austin
LOUISIANA
Baton Rouge
Vicksburg
New Orleans

BATTLES (on map below)
1 Gettysburg
2 Antietam
3 Shenandoah Campaign
4 First and Second Manassas
5 Wilderness
6 Fredericksburg
7 Spotsylvania
8 Chancellorsville
9 Cold Harbor
10 Seven Days' Battles
11 Petersburg
12 Peninsular Campaign
13 First and Second Hampton Roads
PENNSYLVANIA
NEW JERSEY
Harrisburg
Trenton
Gettysburg
OHIO
INDIANA
Columbus
Indianapolis
Antietam
Dover
Annapolis
DELAWARE
WEST VIRGINIA
Washington, D.C.
MARYLAND
Charleston
Frankfort
Richmond
VIRGINIA (enlarged below)
KENTUCKY
Fort Donelson
TENNESSEE
Raleigh
NORTH CAROLINA
Nashville
Shiloh
Chattanooga
Chickamauga
Columbia
SOUTH CAROLINA
Atlanta
ALABAMA
Fort Sumter
Milledgeville
Montgomery
Savannah
GEORGIA
Tallahassee
Mobile Bay
FLORIDA
PENNSYLVANIA
MARYLAND
WEST VIRGINIA admitted to the Union June 20, 1863
Washington, D.C.
Annapolis
VIRGINIA
Richmond
Appomattox

The dead pile up on the Sunken Road at Antietam, September 17, 1862. The carnage in the Civil War was unprecedented.

Quick Facts

- Both Northern and Southern armies were named according to the region where they fought. The Army of the Potomac was headquartered in Washington, D.C., on the banks of the Potomac River. The Army of Northern Virginia was based in Richmond, Virginia. In the West, the Union had the Army of the Cumberland and the Army of the Ohio. The South had the Army of Mississippi and the Army of Tennessee.
- Nineteenth-century armies were generally organized into the following units:
  - Regiments commanded by a colonel. The average Union regiment at Gettysburg was about 350 men.
  - Brigades of two or more regiments, commanded by a brigadier general.
  - Divisions of two or more brigades, commanded by a major general.
  - Corps were made up of divisions. The Union army at Gettysburg had seven infantry corps, each with between 9,000 and 12,000 men. The Confederate army had three infantry corps, each with 20,000 to 22,000 men. Each army also had a corps of cavalry.
- General Meade was given command of the Army of the Potomac just three days before the Battle of Gettysburg. Upon learning of his promotion, he remarked, "Well, I've been tried and convicted without a hearing. I suppose I shall have to go to execution."

Chapter One

The Road to Gettysburg

It was May 1863. The Civil War had raged for two bloody years, and there was no end in sight. When the last of 11 states seceded from the Union in the spring of 1861, no one expected the war to last so long or be so devastating. Southerners labeled the Yankees cowards. Northerners called Southern soldiers lazy. Both sides were wrong. By 1863, tens of thousands of men had already lost their lives, in Virginia, Maryland, Missouri, Kentucky, Mississippi, and Tennessee. Tens of thousands more would lose their lives in the next two years.

The war was making a legend of Confederate general Robert E. Lee. "Marse Robert," as his devoted men called him, was a well-born son of Old Virginia, the son of Revolutionary War hero and Virginia governor Henry "Light Horse Harry" Lee. Lee's reputation at the start of the Civil War was already so high that President Abraham Lincoln offered him the command of the U.S. Army. Even though he had opposed secession, Lee turned Lincoln down. He was a Virginian first and foremost, as he explained to a friend: "I cannot raise my hand against my birthplace, my home, my children." Instead, he became commander of the Confederate Army of Northern Virginia in June 1862 and proceeded to deal a series of crushing blows to the larger and better-equipped Union Army of the Potomac. Lee beat the Federals in the Seven Days' Battles (June 1862), in the Second Battle of Bull Run (August 1862), and at

Fredericksburg (December 1862). Only at Antietam (September 1862) did Lee's army suffer a major defeat.

The Union was not so fortunate with its generals. Commander after commander lost opportunities and misjudged the enemy. President Lincoln was terribly frustrated by his army's failures. Only in the Western theater were Union forces consistently successful. There, Admiral David Farragut captured New Orleans, the most important port on the Mississippi River, and a little-known general named Ulysses S. Grant defeated the Confederates at Shiloh (April 1862). In spring 1863, Grant's troops were closing in on Vicksburg, Mississippi, the last Confederate stronghold on the Mississippi River. If Vicksburg fell, the Confederacy would be cut in half.

The Confederates' latest victory had come at Chancellorsville, Virginia, where from May 1 through May 5, 1863, Lee beat the Union army under General Joseph "Fighting Joe" Hooker. The North lost

Flag officer David Glasgow Farragut. As a reward for his capture of New Orleans, Farragut became the first rear admiral in U.S. history.

The battlefield at Shiloh, where General Ulysses S. Grant won a costly victory for the Union.

Vicksburg, Mississippi, before Grant began his siege of the city in May 1863.

17,000 men. When he heard the news, a horrified President Lincoln burst out, "My God, my God. What will the country say?"

Lincoln was already having a difficult time keeping the country united behind the war. The national mood, upbeat and confident two years before, was now despondent and discouraged. Many people, both in the army and on the home front, now doubted that the North could win. In winter 1863, when spirits were at an all-time low, Captain Oliver Wendell Holmes Jr. wrote, "The army is tired with its hard and terrible experience. I've pretty much made up my mind that the South has achieved their independence." Peace candidates running in federal and state elections in 1863 wanted an immediate end to the war—even if it meant dividing the Union. If these poisonous "Peace Democrats," also known as "Copperheads," won, Lincoln faced opposition to the war in Congress.

But the president knew that times were even harder in the South. The 17,000 men the Union had lost in the Battle of Chancellorsville would soon be replaced by new soldiers. The army's dwindling supplies would be restocked with fresh food and new clothes and ammunition from the North's busy factories. The South, on the other hand, had no easy way to replace its 13,000 casualties—almost a quarter of its army in that battle. Unlike the North, the South did not have an ever-growing immigrant population, nor could it attract black soldiers newly freed by Lincoln's Emancipation Proclamation. The Confederacy had to rely on its existing citizenry for reinforcements. It's no surprise that the rebel army became younger—and older—as the war dragged on.

General Joseph "Fighting Joe" Hooker proved a disappointment at Chancellorsville. When asked why he had failed, he said, "Well, to tell the truth, I just lost confidence in Joe Hooker."

Lee couldn't depend on an ever-renewable fund of armaments and food, either. The few Southern factories in operation were unable to keep up with the demand for guns and ammunition. Confederate soldiers became adept at snatching guns from the dead and wounded. There was not enough food or clothing to go around. Northern troops already occupied much of the best Confederate farmland, and the Union blockades that strangled the Southern coast prevented many foreign ships from entering with provisions. The South was slowly being starved. A clerk in Richmond wrote, "Famine is upon us. I have lost 20 pounds [9 kg], and my wife and children are emaciated."

To make matters even worse, by 1863 Confederate money was almost worthless. Inflation was 12 percent a month. In 1860, the price of a pound (454 g) of salt had been $2. By 1862, it had risen to $60 in some places.

Robert E. Lee knew he was running out of time. The Union was beating the Confederacy in the West. And in the East, the Army of Northern Virginia grew weaker with every victory. It was time for a bold gamble.

Lee would invade the North.

Lincoln reading the Emancipation Proclamation to his cabinet, July 22, 1862. He issued the final proclamation on January 1, 1863, freeing the slaves in the rebellious states.

The move wasn't as desperate as it sounded. Lee knew he couldn't actually conquer the Union states. But if he could win a battle on Northern soil, the North would receive a devastating blow. And by drawing Union troops out of Virginia, away from the Confederate capital at Richmond, he would free Virginia of its invading force. Union troops would no longer be living off Confederate land. Instead, Confederate forces would live off Northern land.

An invasion of the North might have other benefits, too. A victory north of the Mason-Dixon line would threaten Washington, D.C., and President Lincoln would be forced to recall troops from the attack on Vicksburg to defend the capital. Also, a Confederate win would

strengthen the Copperheads. As Lee told Confederate president Jefferson Davis, "We should neglect no honorable means of dividing and weakening our enemies. . . . The most effectual mode of accomplishing this object . . . is to give all encouragement . . . to the rising peace party of the North."

After a short debate, the Confederate government approved the plan. On May 17, Lee started to prepare for his invasion.

President Lincoln didn't know about the invasion—yet. But time was running out for him, too. If the North didn't deliver a major victory soon, he was in deep political trouble. The president had lost confidence in General Hooker, who had completely fallen apart at Chancellorsville. Lincoln decided to replace him with tough military veteran General George Gordon Meade. Meade could be stubborn and bad-tempered. Staff officers called him a "damned old goggle-eyed snapping turtle." But he was also brave, determined, and conscientious. Meade would have to do.

On June 15, the first units of the Confederate Army of Northern Virginia crossed the Potomac River into Maryland. A week and a half later, the Union Army of the Potomac followed. They would meet at the small crossroads town of Gettysburg, Pennsylvania.

Action during the Battle of Chancellorsville. On May 2, 1863, Confederate general "Stonewall" Jackson's men caught Hooker by surprise in a woods known as the Wilderness.

Chapter Two

Fight Like the Devil (Day One)

On June 30, some Confederate soldiers ventured into the small college town of Gettysburg on a foraging expedition. They were looking for shoes, which were in short supply in the rebel army. There they ran into some Union cavalry troops under General John Buford, and they backed out. The next morning, division head Henry Heth decided to go back and get those shoes. Heth told his superior, Third Corps commander A. P. Hill, that Gettysburg was defended by local militia. "I knew they would run as soon as we appeared," Heth later said.

In truth, neither Heth nor anyone else in the Confederate army knew where the Army of the Potomac was. In the 15 days since they had crossed the Mason-Dixon line, Lee and his commanders had lost track of Union forces. Scouting out the Yankees was the job of General "Jeb" Stuart and his cavalry, the "eyes and ears" of the army. But Stuart had taken it upon himself to make a full circle around the Army of the Potomac in order to harass and confuse the enemy. In previous campaigns, Stuart had won renown for his daring "Grand Rounds." This time, he would be disgraced. His showmanship left Lee blind in Union territory.

By June 30, Lee's army was strung out from York, Pennsylvania, to Chambersburg, a distance of approximately 50 miles (80 km). Wherever they went, the Confederate troops caused panic. Yet Lee had given strict orders that no civilians were to be hurt: "We make war only upon

Quick Facts

- ★ The Battle of Gettysburg took place at the height of summer. The fighting day was especially long—from sunup at 4:30 A.M. to sundown at 7:30 P.M.—and temperatures rose into the 90s by mid-afternoon.
- ★ The Iron Brigade was known for its fierce fighting and tall black hats. "Hell, those are not raw militia," a rebel called out when he saw them. "They are those 'black hat' devils!"
- ★ Union brigadier general Francis Barlow was wounded and left paralyzed on July 1 during a skirmish with Confederate brigadier general John B. Gordon's troops. Certain the man would die, Gordon himself offered Barlow a drink of water and promised to send a message to his wife. Incredibly, Barlow survived. He later read that Gordon had died in battle. Fifteen years later, they met by chance at a dinner in Washington, D.C., and were amazed at the other's "resurrection from the dead." They became lifelong friends.
- ★ On Day One at Gettysburg, 12,000 Union troops and 8,000 Confederate troops were killed, wounded, or captured.

armed men," he reminded his troops. Not only that, if the rebels took anything, they were to pay for it—albeit in worthless Confederate money. Towns were overrun by hordes of tattered men in search of food, clothes, and supplies. One girl who watched Confederate cavalry swarm into Gettysburg wrote in her memoirs: "There they were, human beings (!) clad almost in rags, covered with dust, riding wildly; pell-mell down the hill toward our home (!) shouting, yelling most unearthly; cursing, brandishing their revolvers, and firing right and left.

Cavalry commander General John Buford, the first Federal officer to arrive at Gettysburg. He decided to hold the ground until more Union troops could arrive.

Soon the town was filled with infantry, and then the searching and ransacking began in earnest.

"They wanted horses, clothing, anything and almost everything they could conveniently carry away."

The town of Gettysburg was just 12 blocks long and 6 blocks wide, with 2,400 inhabitants. It lay in a gentle valley, surrounded by ridges and hills. Unbeknownst to General Hill, there were no supplies of shoes in town that July 1 morning because shopkeepers had sent most of their goods to Philadelphia before the Confederate scavengers arrived.

Instead, waiting for Heth were U.S. cavalry troops under General John Buford. Buford had arrived in Gettysburg the day before. As soon as he saw Confederate troops in the vicinity, he realized he had to seize the high ground before they did. He stationed his men on McPherson's Ridge, just west of town, and told them the fighting would be tough. "You'll have to fight like the devil until support arrives," he said. In the meantime, Buford sent word to his corps commander, General John F. Reynolds, that Gettysburg was a good place to fight a battle.

At 9:00 A.M. on July 1, 1863, the Battle of Gettysburg began. Buford's dismounted cavalry managed the first assault of Heth's infantry divisions until Reynolds's First Corps could arrive to support them. When Reynolds rode up at about 10:30, he looked over the surrounding hills and ridges and immediately agreed that Gettysburg was prime battlefield material. He wrote to General Meade and called for reinforcements.

Then, Reynolds himself led the Union's famous Iron Brigade into a clash at McPherson's Woods, to the west of the ridge. A few minutes

An 1862 photograph of an Army of the Potomac encampment shows the immense size of the army in the field.

later, a sharpshooter got him in his sights—and Reynolds fell dead, shot through the neck. John Reynolds was the highest-ranking officer to die at Gettysburg.

General Oliver O. Howard, who took over after Reynolds, drove the Confederates from McPherson's Ridge. But their triumph didn't last. Soon General Hill had dispatched the rest of his Confederate corps to back up Heth. By 1:00 P.M., Buford spied Confederate general Richard Ewell's Second Corps arriving from the north. To block his advance, General Howard was forced to swing his troops in a large arc west and north of town, while praying that reinforcements arrived soon. But the Union brigades were overwhelmed. Divided by the massed Confederate onslaught and forced to fall back into town, they fought hand to hand through the streets of Gettysburg. One Union soldier wrote, "The enemy came pouring into town on two if not three sides, and sweeping the streets with a terrific cross fire of musketry." Terrified townspeople hid in their cellars until the fighting was over. By 4:30, the Federals had retreated back to Cemetery Ridge, southeast of town.

When he learned of the hard fighting at Gettysburg that morning, Lee rode east to assess the situation. Since four of his army's nine divisions were still elsewhere, Lee didn't want to have a major engagement that day. But he knew he couldn't leave the Union troops in possession of high ground. So he asked General Ewell to sweep the Federals off Cemetery Hill, "if practicable." It was already late afternoon, and Ewell's men were tired from a hard day's fighting. Ewell decided it was not practicable—so he didn't order an attack.

(opposite): Union troops retreat before a Confederate assault on the first day of battle at Gettysburg. In the foreground, Confederate general John Gordon offers wounded Union general Francis Barlow a drink of water.

When Union general Winfield Scott Hancock arrived at Cemetery Hill at 4:15, he saw "wreck, disaster, disorder. . . . defeat and retreat were everywhere." Yet he also recognized the hill's superb defensive possibilities. Quickly General Hancock sent troops to occupy Culp's

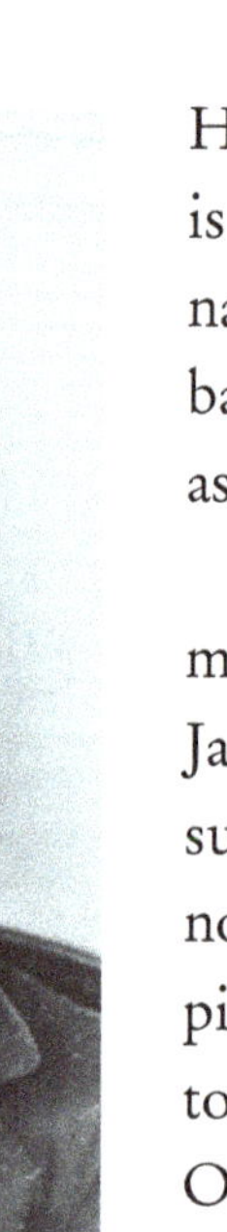

Hill to the northeast. "This is the strongest position by nature up on which to fight a battle that I ever saw," he assured General Howard.

Meanwhile, Lee and his most trusted aide, General James Longstreet, were also surveying the ground. By now the Confederates occupied the high ground west of town, on McPherson's Ridge, Oak Hill, and Seminary Ridge. Longstreet suggested to Lee that the Confederate army should move around to the south and east and cut the Federals off from Washington, D.C. But Lee had smelled victory that day, and his spirits were high. "If the enemy is there tomorrow, we must attack him," he declared.

Lee's optimism was shared by his troops. As a Confederate general later wrote, "Not a man of the entire force present lay down that night with any other expectation than that the next day would witness a crushing defeat of Meade's army."

(left): James Longstreet, the most experienced of Lee's generals at Gettysburg. Lee called him his "old war horse."

(above): General Robert E. Lee was revered by his men and respected by the enemy.

Quick Facts

- On the second day of fighting, the Confederate and Union armies each lost 9,000 men.
- Major General Daniel Sickles was a controversial figure even before Gettysburg. In 1859 he shot and killed Philip Barton Key, the son of the composer of "The Star-Spangled Banner," because Key had been having an affair with Sickles's wife. Sickles was found not guilty on the basis of temporary insanity—and was even reconciled with his wife!
- Colonel Joshua Lawrence Chamberlain remained with the Army of the Potomac for the duration of the war, although he was wounded four times. He had the honor of receiving the Confederate surrender at Appomattox. After the war, he became president of Bowdoin College and governor of Maine.
- In the assault on Cemetery Hill, Confederate colonel Isaac Avery was struck in the throat by a bullet. As he was dying, he scribbled a final message to his friend Major Sam Tate: "Major, tell my Father I died with my face to the Enemy. I. E. Avery." The note was still clutched in his hand when his body was found.

Chapter Three:

A Fearful Destruction (Day Two)

General George Meade arrived at the battlefield in the early hours of July 2, exhausted from travel and eager to see the field for himself. A steady stream of Union forces followed him. By late morning, General Meade had nearly 90,000 men under his command. He positioned them along a mile-long (1.6 km) defensive front shaped like a giant fishhook, stretching from Culp's Hill in the north to Cemetery Hill and down the length of Cemetery Ridge. The shaft of the hook ended in the south at two hills known as Little Round Top and Big Round Top.

General George Gordon Meade, commander of the Army of the Potomac at Gettysburg.

In the center of the Union line, where Cemetery Hill and Cemetery Ridge joined, Meade positioned his major artillery units. The ground was defended by the First and Second Corps and by the newly arrived Fifth Corps. On the southern shaft of the fishhook, the Third Corps was supposed to take the left flank of the Union line.

But Major General Daniel Sickles decided not to stay on Cemetery Ridge. In search of more favorable high ground, he advanced his men half a mile (800 m) in front of the line. His controversial decision left the Union left flank open to attack.

Lee also rose before dawn to finalize his plans for the day. His 75,000 troops surrounded the Union army on three sides, along a six-mile (9.5 km) arc. His plan was to have Ewell's Second Corps attack Culp's Hill, the Union right flank, in the north. He ordered a reluctant General Longstreet to attack Meade's vulnerable left flank.

By 10:00 in the morning, Lee's plans were firm. Some experts think that if Longstreet had attacked at once, before all Union forces were in

The struggle for Devil's Den, an area of rocky terrain beneath Little Round Top.

Major General John Bell Hood commanded Longstreet's right-hand division on July 2. He was wounded early in the attack and left the field.

place, the Confederates would have had the advantage. But "Old Pete," always cautious, did not move until Major General John Bell Hood's brigade had arrived. Thus it was not until 4:00 in the afternoon that the second day's fighting began.

Hood moved against Sickles's troops, now occupying a peach orchard and a rocky area called Devil's Den in front of the Union line. The fight was fierce, as one Union colonel later remembered: "On both sides, each [soldier] aimed at his man, and men fell dead and wounded with frightful rapidity." Sickles himself was wounded, shot by a Confederate cannon, and had to have a leg amputated. (In later years he would visit his severed leg bone at the Army Medical Museum in Washington, D.C.) Hood, too, ended up with a shattered arm.

Hood's men were about to climb Little Round Top when Meade's chief engineer, Brigadier General Gouverneur K. Warren, noticed that

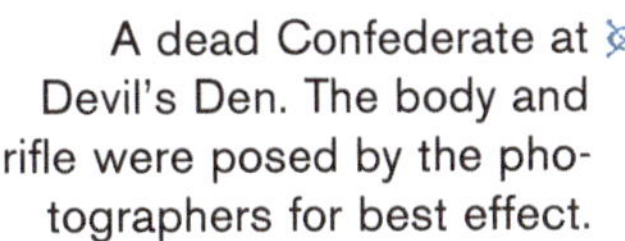

A dead Confederate at Devil's Den. The body and rifle were posed by the photographers for best effect.

no one was defending it. He rushed in a brigade led by Colonel Strong Vincent and told him to hold the hill. Vincent got his regiments into position just in time. Fifteen minutes later, the Confederates stormed the slope.

The eastern side of the hill was defended by the 20th Maine Volunteer Infantry, commanded by a language professor named Colonel Joshua Lawrence Chamberlain. Chamberlain was ordered to hold his position—the extreme end of the mile-long (1.6 km) Union line—"at all hazard." The 500 soldiers of the 15th Alabama flung themselves at the hill and were repulsed again and again by 385 stubborn Yankees. At last, as the 20th Maine was running out of powder and cannonballs, the desperate Chamberlain seized the initiative. "Bayonet!" he shouted. With one accord, his men fixed bayonets to their rifles and charged down the hill. Startled, the Alabamians fled or surrendered.

Colonel Joshua Lawrence Chamberlain was the intrepid commander of the 20th Maine.

In this one encounter, the 20th Maine lost a third of its men; the 15th Alabama lost half. It was a fearful cost. A soldier from the 20th Maine remembered, "Not only on the crest of the hill among the bluecoats was blood running in little rivulets and forming crimson pools, but in the gray ranks . . . there had also been fearful destruction."

It was even harder for Union troops to protect the western slope of Little Round Top. Colonel Strong Vincent was mortally wounded while trying to rally his troops against two Confederate brigades. To ward off the coming onslaught, General Gouverneur Warren again grabbed a passing regiment and sent it off to the top of the hill. In the end, Little Round Top remained in Union hands.

Sickles was not so fortunate. His troops were pushed back. Around 6:00 P.M., an Alabama brigade charged the gap in Union lines where Sickles's corps was supposed to have been. In literally a stopgap measure, General Hancock ordered 262 Minnesotans to attack the 1,600

Alabamians. Despite the hopeless odds, the gallant regiment fixed bayonets and charged. When the assault was over, only 47 men of the First Minnesota returned to the Federal line. But by then more reinforcements had arrived, and the Union center was saved.

General Ewell's Confederate forces in the north were supposed to take advantage of Longstreet's assault in the south to take Culp's Hill. But Ewell's assault was badly coordinated, and by nightfall only one brigade had managed to seize some trenches left vacant by a departed Federal unit.

A pencil sketch of the battle on Culp's Hill drawn by a participant.

(opposite): Federal field ambulances for transporting wounded. Both sides tried to collect their wounded after each day's fighting, but sometimes the injured had to wait for attention until the whole battle was over.

And so ended the second day of fighting at Gettysburg. It had been a day of many individual battles, of enormous bravery and great sacrifice on both sides. Again and again the initiative and quick thinking of Union officers had saved the day for the North. On the Confederate side, however, bad timing and lack of coordination had resulted in stalemate and frustration. The Union line had not broken, and Federal troops still held Cemetery Ridge, Culp's Hill, and the Round Tops. As Longstreet had feared, the Confederates had suffered great losses without winning a victory.

The total casualties for the two days were nearly 35,000, making Gettysburg the bloodiest engagement of the war thus far. And the battle wasn't over yet.

Detail of Paul Philippoteaux's famous cyclorama painting which depicts the third day of the Battle of Gettysburg. The Federal artillery is firing on advancing Confederate troops.

Chapter Four

The Last Full Measure (Day Three)

That night, an uneasy peace descended over the battlefield. Soldiers on both sides gathered around campfires for a bite to eat and a cup of coffee, then settled down to catch a few hours of sleep before daybreak. "The stillness," as one Federal officer recalled, "was only broken by the moans of the wounded yet uncared for in our front."

At Union headquarters Meade met with his generals to determine the next day's strategy. Should Union forces go on the attack or defend the ground they already held? The decision was unanimous: They would hold the line where they were. Meade expressed the opinion that if Lee struck again, it would be in the center of his line, on Cemetery Ridge.

The center was not Lee's first choice of attack, however. Before dawn on July 3, he saddled his horse and rode south along Seminary Ridge to confer with Longstreet. Lee's plan called for Longstreet's corps to repeat the tactics of the day before: pound the Union right flank while Ewell assailed the left flank at Culp's Hill. Longstreet did not agree with that strategy. The divisions that had fought the previous day were spent. Instead, Longstreet wanted to go south around the Round Tops and attack the Union line from the rear.

To Lee, that tactic sounded too much like a retreat. He had another

Quick Facts

- Confederate general Lewis Armistead and Union general Winfield Scott Hancock were good friends before the war. After Armistead was shot, he learned that Hancock, too, had been wounded. His last words were, "Tell General Hancock I am sorry." Armistead died, but Hancock survived to run for president in 1880. He lost by a narrow margin to James Garfield.
- After the war, Longstreet wrote, "My heart was heavy. I could see the desperate and hopeless nature of the charge and the hopeless slaughter it would cause. . . . That day at Gettysburg was one of the saddest of my life."
- Pickett never forgave Lee for the events of July 3. "That old man," he would say, "had my division massacred."
- Some 7,500 Confederate soldiers were killed, wounded, or captured in Pickett's charge. The Federals had only 1,500 casualties.
- The total casualties (killed, wounded, captured, and missing) at Gettysburg were 23,000 for the Union army and 28,000 for the Confederate army.
- More than 3,000 horses died at Gettysburg.
- Only one Gettysburg civilian died during the battle—20-year-old Jennie Wade, who was shot by a stray bullet on July 3 while baking biscuits in her sister's home on Cemetery Hill.

idea. He knew that Union soldiers from Cemetery Ridge had been shifted to reinforce troops in the north and south. The center of the line must therefore be the Union's weakest, most vulnerable spot. The Confederates would attack the center.

The assault that Lee proposed would become the most famous action of the Civil War. Eleven Confederate infantry brigades led by General George E. Pickett would march three-quarters of a mile (1.2 km) from Seminary Ridge across an open field to Cemetery Ridge. To take out Union guns ahead of time, Confederate artillery would bombard the Union lines for an hour before the assault.

The march would become known as Pickett's charge.

Longstreet was dismayed by the idea. Years later, he wrote that he told Lee, "General, I have been a soldier all my life. . . . It is my opinion that no 15,000 men ever arrayed for battle can take that position."

But Lee was adamant. He believed the assault would work because, as he admitted later, he thought his men were "invincible." Yet the idea of a full frontal attack over open ground was already out of date when Lee proposed it. The deadly precision of 19th-century rifles and artillery practically guaranteed that the advancing troops would be mowed

General "Jeb" Stuart, commander of the cavalry of the Army of Northern Virginia.

down before they could reach their objective. Tragically, even 50 years later, the generals of World War I would order their soldiers to make the same hopeless, suicidal attacks.

Pickett's charge would not be the only action of July 3. In the north, the Federals would drive the Confederates off Culp's Hill after seven hours of attacks and counterattacks. In the south, Confederate general Jeb Stuart would attempt to lead his cavalry in an assault on the Union rear, only to be halted by a Federal division. But it was Pickett's charge that decided the battle.

The temperature on Cemetery Ridge had climbed to a sultry 89 °F (31 °C) by early afternoon. Just after 1:00, the 160 guns of the rebel army let loose with an earsplitting barrage. A Gettysburg resident later wrote, "All felt that this day must decide who should conquer. . . . That afternoon the cannonading began. . . . such cannonading no one ever heard. Nothing can be compared to it, one who has never heard it cannot form any idea how terrible it is." The volley could be heard as far away as Pittsburgh. Yet for all the thunderous boom, the Union guns were not knocked out, for the Confederate artillery aimed too high.

On Seminary Ridge, Pickett and his men impatiently waited for the command to advance. At last, at 3:00, a resistant Longstreet gave the order. In closely packed ranks, 13,000 soldiers marched along a front almost a mile (1.6 km) wide. It was a magnificent sight, never to be forgotten by those who witnessed it. A Union officer described the advance as an "overwhelming resistless tide of an ocean of armed men sweeping upon us! On they move, as with one soul in perfect order . . . magnificent, grim, irresistible."

And doomed.

Confederate infantry marches across the open field towards Cemetery Ridge at the start of Pickett's charge.

The Union guns waited until the rebel infantry was within 1,200 yards (1,097 m); then they opened fire. As many as a dozen men fell with every shot, blasted by shells and canisters of musket balls. Soon the field was covered with the dead and wounded. Incredibly, the men still came onward at a regulation walk, about 100 yards (91 m) a minute. But the gallant Confederate line began to break down. Only half the original force made it across the road in front of Cemetery Ridge. With a defiant rebel yell, some of Pickett's men charged toward a low stone wall at the center of the Union line.

The only Confederate general to reach that wall, Lewis Armistead, swung his hat on top of his sword and called out, "Come on, boys! Give them the cold steel. Who will follow me?" About 150 men came after him, charging toward the Federal artillery. A minute later, Armistead was down, felled by rifle fire. Those few daring men who broke the Union line with him were also captured or killed. The place where Armistead was killed was the "high-water mark" of the advance.

Placing his hat on his sword and waving it over his head, General Lewis Armistead rushes toward the Union battery on Cemetery Hill. His action was the climax—and final defeat—of Pickett's charge.

The Confederate assault was over. All along the Confederate line, soldiers began to surrender or retreat. Of the 13,000 men who had set out, fewer than half stumbled back to Seminary Ridge. A dazed Pickett watched the retreat from his observation post behind the lines. When Lee told him to regroup his division in case of counterattack, Pickett said simply, "General, I have no division now." He had lost two-thirds of his men.

Lee blamed himself for the rout. "It's all my fault. It is I who have lost this fight," he said to the survivors. For the rest of the afternoon and into the evening, he waited for a counterassault. But it never came. The Union troops, jubilant but exhausted, had had enough for the day.

That night General Pickett wrote an agonized letter to his fiancée: "I can still hear them [his soldiers] cheering as I gave the order, 'Forward!' The Thrill of their joyous voices as they called out, 'We'll follow you, Marse [master] George, we'll follow you!' On, how faithfully they followed me on, on to their death, and I led them on, on, on, oh God!"

General Meade and the Army of the Potomac had won the Battle of Gettysburg.

Chapter Five

This Hallowed Ground

The day after the battle was a scene of unimaginable chaos. In a letter to his wife, a captain from 20th Maine described the horror of it: "Heaven save you from the distress of such scenes. Blackened and mangled corpses—dead horses—guns and equipment broken and strewn . . . and an almost unbearable stench—confusion all about—burning the dead—hauling away wounded, etc., etc. Oh, what scenes."

Lee and Meade faced each other, waiting for someone to make the first move. Lee knew it was time to retreat. Late in the afternoon of July 4, he started to send his wagon train of wounded—17 miles (27 km) long—southwest under cover of blinding rain. Later that night, the infantry began to move out.

Meade started in pursuit the next day. But he was slow, the weather was bad, and the Confederates had a head start. When the Federals finally caught up with Lee on the banks of the Potomac, Meade's generals argued about whether to attack. While they delayed, Lee and his army slipped across the Potomac into Virginia.

President Lincoln was furious with Meade for letting Lee escape. "To have closed upon [Lee] would, in connection with our other late successes, have ended the war," Lincoln wrote to Meade in an angry letter. "As it is, the war is prolonged indefinitely. . . . Your golden

(opposite): Dead men and horses litter the ground at Gettysburg. Ghastly scenes like this were repeated over the whole battlefield.

opportunity is gone." Having vented his feelings, Lincoln put the letter in his pocket and never sent it. He couldn't afford to lose Meade.

Confederate president Jefferson Davis couldn't afford to lose his commander, either, and when Lee tried to resign in shame and despair, Davis refused to let him do it. And so the Army of the Potomac and the Army of Northern Virginia once again made camp in Virginia, five miles (8 km) from each other on either side of the Rappahannock River. They seemed to be back where they had started two months before.

Jefferson Davis, president of the Confederacy, was greatly disappointed in the outcome at Gettysburg. But he would not accept Lee's offer to resign.

Yet the momentum of the war had changed. Four days after Gettysburg, Lincoln received a telegram from General Grant reporting the fall of Vicksburg. The victories at Vicksburg and Gettysburg were the turning point of the Civil War. Today we can look back and see that the "high-water mark" on Cemetery Ridge was the beginning of the end for the Confederacy.

For the surviving soldiers of both armies, the Battle of Gettysburg was over. But it was not over on the killing fields themselves, where the dead lay in the hot July sun. A Confederate prisoner pressed into burial service wrote, "The sights and smells that assailed us were indescribable—corpses swollen to twice their original size, some of them actually burst asunder." Army burial squads worked night and day, quickly burying the corpses of men and horses in shallow graves. Decomposing bodies continued to surface all summer long, forcing residents to carry handkerchiefs dipped in vinegar to block the smell of rotting flesh.

The small town was quite overwhelmed by the immensity of the tragedy. Even the wounded outnumbered Gettysburg's population by ten to one. After 300 surgeons had amputated limbs for a week, a teenager recalled seeing a "pile of limbs higher than a fence" right by her front door.

Clearly something had to be done. The dead deserved a dignified burial, and the civilians needed relief from the trauma they had endured. The governor of Pennsylvania contacted the governors of the 17 other Union states that also had soldiers die in the battle, and together they raised the money for a proper burial ground. The dedication of the Gettysburg National Cemetery was set for November 19, 1863.

The main speaker at the ceremony would be Edward Everett, a distinguished statesman and renowned orator. President Lincoln was also invited to formally dedicate the cemetery and make "a few appropriate remarks." He worked on his speech in Washington, D.C., scribbling the first 19 lines on White House stationery. He finished it on the night of November 18 after he arrived in Gettysburg.

A doctor performs an amputation in a hospital field tent. Amputation was the most common method of treatment for a bullet wound because most doctors did not have the ability or time to repair wounds surgically.

Hospital tents at Gettysburg, July 1863. Casualties were so severe that such tent cities were not sufficient to hold the wounded. Most of the buildings in the city were used as hospitals for months.

Lincoln didn't want to recite a formal history of the battle; he knew Everett would do that. He wanted to remind people why the battle had been fought: so that the United States and the principles on which it had been founded would endure.

The audience cheered Everett's two-hour oration. They seemed less enthusiastic about Lincoln's brief address. But many contemporaries immediately recognized its brilliance. Everett himself sent Lincoln a congratulatory note: "I should be glad if I could flatter myself that I came as near to the central idea of the occasion in two hours as you did in two minutes."

Today the Gettysburg Address is recognized as a masterpiece of the English language and one of the most important speeches in American history.

In 1863, Edward Everett of Massachusetts was one of the most famous speakers in the United States.

The scene at the dedication of the National Cemetery where Lincoln delivered the Gettysburg Address. Lincoln is seated in the center, to the left of the man in the top hat.

★ The Gettysburg Address ★

Four score and seven years ago our fathers brought forth, on this continent, a new nation, conceived in liberty and dedicated to the proposition that all men are created equal.

Now we are engaged in a great civil war, testing whether that nation, or any nation so conceived and so dedicated, can long endure. We are met on a great battlefield of that war. We have come to dedicate a portion of that field, as a final resting place for those who here gave their lives, that this nation might live. It is altogether fitting and proper that we should do this.

But in a larger sense, we cannot dedicate—we cannot consecrate—we cannot hallow this ground. The brave men, living and dead, who struggled here, have consecrated it far above our poor power to add or subtract. The world will little note, nor long remember, what we say here, but it can never forget what they did here. It is for us the living, rather, to be dedicated here to the unfinished work which they who fought here have thus far so nobly advanced. It is rather for us the living to be here dedicated to the great task remaining before us—that from these honored dead we take increased devotion to that cause for which they here gave the last full measure of devotion—that we here highly resolve that these dead shall not have died in vain—that this nation, under God, shall have a new birth of freedom—and that government of the people, by the people, for the people, shall not perish from the earth.

Further Reading

Beller, Susan P. *To Hold This Ground: A Desperate Battle at Gettysburg.* New York: Simon & Schuster, 1995.

Corrick, James A. *The Battle of Gettysburg.* San Diego: Lucent Books, 1996.

Feinberg, Barbara Silberdick. *Abraham Lincoln's Gettysburg Address.* Brookfield, Conn.: Twenty-First Century Books, 2000.

Hakim, Joy. *War, Terrible War: A History of Us.* New York: Oxford University Press, 1994.

Katcher, Philip. *The Civil War Source Book.* New York: Facts on File, 1992.

Marrin, Jim. *Commander-in-Chief Abraham Lincoln and the Civil War.* New York: Dutton, 1997.

McPherson, James. *Fields of Fury.* New York: Atheneum, 2002.

Murphy, Jim. *The Long Road to Gettysburg.* New York: Clarion, 1992.

Shaara, Michael. *The Killer Angels.* New York: David McKay, 1974. Reprint, New York: Ballantine, 1975.

Glossary

Amputation—The surgical removal of a limb or appendage.

Army of Northern Virginia—Confederate Army stationed in Northern Virginia.

Army of the Potomac—Union army stationed along the banks of the Potomac River.

Artillery—Weapons, like cannons, that discharge missiles; also the branch of an army armed with artillery.

Bayonet—A steel blade attached to a rifle and used in hand-to-hand combat.

Blockade—The blocking of an enemy shore or harbor by warships or troops.

Brigade—A large body of troops made up of two or more regiments and commanded by a brigadier general.

Casualty—A soldier who is killed, wounded, or missing.

Cavalry—The branch of an army that is mounted on horseback.

Confederate—A person who was a citizen of the Confederate States of America.

Confederate States of America—The name of the nation formed by the 11 states that seceded from the United States in 1860 and 1861.

Constitutional Convention (1787)—The meeting of delegates in Philadelphia who wrote a constitution for the United States.

Copperheads—Northerners who wanted to compromise with the Confederates and end the Civil War.

Corps—A tactical unit of the army made up of two or more divisions.

Cotton gin—A machine invented by Eli Whitney in 1793 to clean cotton fibers.

Division—A military unit composed of three to five brigades.

Emancipation Proclamation (1863)—President Lincoln's declaration freeing the slaves in the Confederacy.

Gettysburg Address (1863)—The speech given by President Lincoln after the Battle of Gettysburg.

Infantry—The branch of an army composed of soldiers who fight on foot.

Mason-Dixon Line—Imaginary line between the Northern and Southern states.

Militia—An army of citizens with no officially trained soldiers who serve during an emergency.

Musket—A shoulder gun carried by the infantry.

Peace Democrats—Northern Democrats during the Civil War who wanted peace at any price.

Regiment—A military unit of about 350 troops, usually commanded by a colonel.

Revolutionary War (1776-83)—The war fought by the 13 states against Great Britain for American independence.

Secede—To withdraw from or leave an organization.

Secessionist—In the Civil War, someone who believed in the right of a state to separate from the United States.

Slavery—The state of one person being owned by another.

Union—During the Civil War, the states that did not secede from the United States of America.

Index

www.ingramcontent.com/pod-product-compliance
Lightning Source LLC
Chambersburg PA
CBHW040853100426
42813CB00015B/2792

* 9 7 8 1 5 9 6 8 7 7 2 4 5 *